WHERE EVERYTHING WILD HAS A HOME

WILD POEMS

Where Everything Wild Has a Home

Wild Poems

Christine McDonald

Library of Congress Cataloging in Publishing Data is
available.
ISBN 979-8-9854448-0-3

Cover Design and Logo © by Christine McDonald
Editing by Katia Ariel
Author Photo: Ross Photography

For the wildness in all beings

Table of Contents

An Introduction and An Invitation

I was born in the wild and come from the wild. When I walk in a forest I wonder if the sap in the trees is any different than the blood in my veins. I care deeply about the wild because of my early childhood bonds with nature and animals, and because of the way I feel when I watch swallows riding the wind, the budding of spring blooms or the pause I feel in my heart beating in harmony with yours.

The heart of this book began in 2019 when my husband and I left our home of thirty years on the Oregon Coast and moved to a small farm in eastern Washington. I felt called to be on this land by the trees, the river, and the spirits of the hills, but change can be unsettling. We took down fences, expanded the gardens to be able to live sustainably, and began planting trees and shrubs along the river and hillside to nurture habitat for the wild animals. Writing these poems grounded me and like a compass needle oriented me to my true north again and again during these disorienting times. Less than a year after our arrival the world had changed significantly. Not just for humans but the animals we desired to help. Deer populations have waned, songbirds have declined throughout the northwest, bees are threatened by herbicides and insecticides, and habitat area dwindles as subdivisions grow. The list of species stressed, threatened, or going extinct grows every day. The wild animals, forests, mountains, prairies, and rivers we took for granted in our youth are disappearing rapidly.

In the fall of 2021, a deer died within our fenced garden area. How and why the deer managed to get behind the fence and into our garden is a mystery. For weeks I pondered the event and came to realize that I too had put up a fence of denial to protect myself from the scale of loss in these extraordinary times.

This was a wakeup call to allow the garden of my heart to experience the loss of species on a local and global scale. My spiritual Teacher Leslie Temple Thurston would tell us death is a doorway and loss is an illusion. The death of the deer taught me the beauty of things shines beneath the brokenness. As we grow into the loss, not away from it, resilience is gained. Below all the pain, suffering, and grief I trust my wild resilience to find the way. I believe that each visitation into the bottom of hardship brings us closer to a softer and stronger core within. Trusting in the resilience of life is what makes the wild WILD and connects humans to wild species. This collection of poems continues to be a source of guidance and connection for me.

At the beginning of each chapter, I have included an invitation to the reader on how these poems can guide you to finding your own wild connection. Let your focus broaden into the wilderness of your soul as you read them. These poems are my love poems to nature, the animals the trees and to you.

Wild Writings

An Invitation: You have a wilderness that exists within you. This wild place is filled with wonder, beauty and diversity and can be found within regardless of your surroundings. These poems get to call you from the busy, mind driven world back to your heart of wilderness. In this way the wild lives.

Wild Calling

You don't have to be wild
You can be as tame as a bird in a cage,
debating the length of your wings,
or the purpose of trees.

But maybe, just once, put up a squawk,
and when the door opens, cut loose
and take flight in any direction
but the one you came from.

Darling, you don't have to believe me—
it is better if you don't.
But trust yourself—
you were meant to be free.

Freedom is independence from an outcome.
When you stop looking for its source,
freedom meets you at the door.

You don't have to do anything
but stare at the white space on this page
and wonder how wild
you can BE.

Consumed

bring all of you into the forest
to be consumed
by the sharp needles of spruce
the long silhouette of pines
the tender fronds of unfurling ferns

let yourself be consumed-
by the beauty of trees
the chatter of squirrels
the stillness of a lake
the speed of a bear

to be devoured, expended or used up
by everything bigger or smaller
than the tender form of self
in the rough hands of our humanness

is to lose everything
in the not-so-big house
of God

Where All That Is Wild Has a Home

One more elephant, one more whale,
one more polar bear, or frog, or lily
until none remain. Extinction
is no longer imagined or distant.

The gold has lost its luster.
I am coming down from the yellow mountain
before color dissolves and grays another horizon.

Hello belly, hello body, hello toes.
No matter where I go
my feet touch the earth.

My whole body is supported
by a whole planet.
Where all that is wild has a home.
In the shadows
of the valleys of gold
rides a wild woman.

She is calling my name, calling me home.
Together we're going to ride out of that valley,
sparking a fire that outshines the gold.

Here in the palm of my hand, in the wrinkle of my skin,
in the shine of my eyes, there is a wildfire
giving rise to a world where women and animals
are valued for something other than their parts.

Wolf Song

Last night I heard of the wolf
in the barnyard.

The land that grew me is still wild,
maybe even wilder now.

Wolves and grizzly bears once hunted
have returned with the help of society.

I have never seen a wolf in the wild,
so I imagine it.

Hiding under a dented Chevy pickup,
fearful of the barking dogs.

Too young, or maybe too hungry
to know the dangers.

A cold wind blows
the scent of humans and metal.

The young grayish female
makes a run for the dense willows in the valley.

Did the wolf pay
for this rare visitation?

My heart is dreaming of a time
when the mystery of the wild lives.

Smoke

You awaken to the smell of smoke.
The smell drifts through the night, demanding
your attention. There is a strange feeling,
insisting you get out of bed.

The air is cool, but your skin
is warmed by a winter breeze.
There is no smoke.

The moon with her soft radiance
outlines layered hills of silt
and pointed silhouettes
of ancient ponderosa pines
casting a halo on the raging river below.

There is a flooding of voices
coming from the hawthorn thicket.
You stare into the darkness with fear and curiosity.
The sound gets louder until you hear words.

"We smell you! We smell you! We smell you!"
You feel the pull of caves and wild hollows in the earth
and primal voices speaking the language of wolves.
If you stay you will be eaten by the fear.

You run, pull into the body's awareness
that this is a dream. An invitation from the soul.
You know you will say yes even as the fear
consumes your flesh.

Lonely Warrior

My loneliness is a warrior.
Willing to go to battle
until she stands alone,
defeated by her own desolation.

As a child I took comfort knowing that the warrior
of my heart tended to my grief.
I took refuge in her strength,
knowing the safety of her boundaries.

I honor her.
I see her.
I grieve for her.

I rejoice in her aliveness
as she gives up her territory
in the slip of a hand.
The other is outstretched to you.

The reader, the friend,
or the stranger on the street
to land in the tender humility
of your own warrior heart.

Child Wild

Time to push, stretch,
let myself go to the wild side of me.

Stepping to the left and then the right,
a rhythm finds its way under my skin.

The eyes follow my toes to the floor,
hunting for earth harmony.
The knees bend and sway
and start a movement up my legs
to the booty of my spine.

Now there is no stopping
the flow of emotion
from that wild animal in me.

The vibration of something
older than this body comes alive.
Dancing to the rhythm of a primal heart,
this child of the universe wakes up.

"Child Wild!" she screams
from the depth of her toes to a cosmic sky.
"Follow me -If you dare!"

A New Fire Story

Before there were bears there were mountains.
Before there were mountains there was fire.

Fire everywhere-
in the molten rock pouring forth new earth
upward and outward until mountains met skyline
to be cooled by the breath of stars
silhouetting earths magnificent expression in rocky ridgelines
where bears now find refuge.

I cannot imagine a world without bears
or mountains-the two intwined in the tapestry
of fire, rocky precipices and sharp claws.

Before the mountain trail there was the grizzly
eyes seeing right though me
into the mitochondrial fire of my being
re-awakening the wonder of wonder.

Before wonder
there was nothing
not even fire.

We live on a planet of wonder and awe.

We have traveled a long way over mountains
and valleys in fear of fire and wonder.

To see life through the eyes of a bear
is to know the deep peace of mountains.

The peace we seek can be found
in the mystery of the fire of wonder.

Fire and *Water*

I. Fire

2021 was the year the amygdala
        was repeatedly traumatized by "The News."
Fear, fear, and more fear
        until our bellies were full of dread,

our hearts masked,
        our minds distanced from the truth.
The year of *not my reality*.
        The year two plus one equated to zero.

The year a new direction
        became crystal clear.
The year where survival meant
        find your bliss.

For this is a fire time
        of finding your family of frequency.
A new north is birthing
        in the wild smoke.

Take a breath—
        there is a blaze burning within.
The dragon of revolution and regeneration,
        creation and chaos have gone viral.

II. Water

Sipping water—calming the fire within.
        Not just any water but the water of ceremony.
Water anchored into the earth and sun
        and all that resides between.

Infused with intention as I surrender to the authorship
        of my essence where lifeblood and soul intertwine.
I am writing a chapter on staying conscious, grounded
        as the world changes, shifts, and transforms.

In another chapter I am water flowing
        with the energies and cycles
of the earth, plants, animals, water, the sun and moon,
        and my own creative substance.

In this year of twos, I play with the fluidity of relationship
        freeing love and joy into long lasting memories.
Within the hidden depth of water
        I mother an inner warrior.

For I am a wild thing at heart as mysterious
        as the silver lining of gratitude after a storm.
The birthing and honoring of an electric essence
        is shooting from the stars.

Vaporizing like dew on the glass
        of purified water
now crystallized
        on my tongue.

What a Wild Thing Knows

There is wilderness in every person.
Wild things trust the body
where a jungle of pure creativity
hides in the shadow of form.

All that is wild lives according
to natural wisdom and laws.
What is wild has guided humanity
through unknown territory.

Lions and bears, viruses and bacteria,
natural disasters, big and small,
feed the wisdom of evolution.

The container is ready to burst.
If you listen, you can hear
the roar.

Reverence

An Invitation: Reverence wakes up our connection to what we care about. Reverence is an internal prayer-an inner dialogue with the SELF that sets the stage for how we relate to our bodies, relationships, and our surroundings. Let these words guide you to a state of awe and reverence for all things.

How to Begin Each Day

Before you open your eyes
open your heart.

Before one muscle moves
be grateful for just one thing.

Before your feet touch the ground
feel the pull of the earth grounding you to this day.

Before one step is taken
Remember that very first step that was not taken for granted.

Pausing before the door opens, the car starts, or words
are spoken is a form of yielding.

Yielding to the creator within ripples out like water
on a pond until love is the only thing to stop for.

That is how the heart
taught me to yield.

A Forest Prayer

When I walk in a forest
I see each tree as a guest
around a table of earth and rock.

I focus on a single tree
streaming green light through clustered needles,
my eyes adjusting and filtering
so my heart will not explode,
splinter, and turn to ash.

I sit at the table
humbled by the wind combing branches
and scattering needles
over a rich microbiome beneath my feet.

Soft brown lichens are etched in bark,
roots nourished by miles of fungi
all in harmony to some song I cannot hear
but know exists.

I desire to be more like the pines
above my head,
their cores expanding and contracting
like my breath.

I send a prayer to my toes to take root
and ground this offering.
The agitation of thought dissolves
into a simple question:

"What if nature expands in awareness
as I expand in awareness?"

What if our unity alters entropy
and protons and neutrons reorganize,
expanding the crown of trees
beyond my imagination?

A child in Seattle or Singapore
looks up from a screen and sees a tree looking back
and gazes into the green light filtering through leaves
and knows she is not alone.

And we sit around the table
seeing each other
for the first
time.

A River Runs Free

In a narrow constriction of the valley floor
a wall of rock and cement over eighty feet high
dissolves like dust and a river runs free.

From the top of the ridge above the Old Mill Pond
the toy-like dump trucks, excavators, and backhoes
hold no comparison to the river's power, ease, and grace.

The river awakens something within me.
Is this what the passion of freedom feels like?
To face the pillars of the past and blast through the walls
of withholding and withdrawing until only dust remains.

The river freed has touched a nerve in my heart,
which sends a pulse to widen the chambers of love.
The belly softens and tears drop quietly to the earth.

The life force of the river and my life force unite
as we meander across
the raw landscape of this moment.

RedBird

Before the journey to RedBird we fell into the familiar pit
of right and wrong and no one wins, repeating
a thirty-year pattern just because we know it so well.

Needing an escape, we drove down
the winding highway of the Lewiston grade
to a new trail, RedBird.

RedBird was once home to the Nez Perce Indians
before sheep and cattle descended the canyon walls
to the narrow floodplain along RedBird Creek.

From the top of the ridge, the hills roll and twist
as if the goddess of the Snake River
has had her say in their making.
Snow dusts the hilltops on this cool April morning.
As we enter the canyon, the unwinding begins.

At mile one, springs and streams overflowing
their banks soften the silence between us.

At mile two, the coolness of conflict fades
into the warmth of the rocky canyon.

At mile three, the unspoken beauty
begins to wear down the feelings of separation.

At mile four, I feel myself attune to the ancient spirits of
RedBird. A gradual stillness settles over me.

At mile five, RedBird Canyon opens to the heart of the Snake
River.
As we stop to rest, I hear a whisper:
"Sometimes it takes a journey down before
the song in your heart returns to the surface."

First Snow

This morning and yesterday
fresh snow came down in big, soft flakes
that wet my nose, grayed my orange puffer jacket
and landed in my mouth, where I savored the softness.

It felt like the first experience of snow.
As if some miracle had just happened—
everything was covered with deepening
white silence.

The kind of silence that stops thought, not to mention cars.
The kind of silence that slows down legs of every size
and makes you want to touch the space between
each miraculous drop of life.

The mystery melts in the palm of my hand
as I realize what is most precious
is transitory and can only be seen from
my own inner wilderness of stillness.

Summer Soul Haibun*

There is sweetness in the summer heat. The hillside browns in shades of oatgrass yellow, clumps of fescues wave their slender stems as the wheat nods its heavy head in a bow to a creator. The sunflowers lengthen their stalks, capturing rays of sun to add to their collection. Water becomes the essential nutrient as I drink its many forms before making my own. The neighborhood stargazers find a common thread in the dusk, releasing the pursuit for altered illumination.

For me the sweetest part of the sun's eventual surrender is those late nights when the stars linger as they gaze down on me. My heart swells like the moon in her fullness and beams back my own celestial light. For I am a summer soul at heart. When I reach back into the mirror of this life I will hold the silver lining of summer heat in the shadows of time.

The moon softens
the bright solar
light of my existence.

* *The haibun form is a concentrated prose block that ends with a whisper in the form of haiku. This haibun was inspired by Aimee Nezhukumatathil's, "Summer Haibun."*

Heart Opening

One week after open-heart surgery
my brother texts me:
"Got Covid—asymptomatic.
They are going to keep me here a few more days."

Two weeks after the open-heart surgery
he goes home with help,
family help,
my help.

Three weeks after my brother's open-heart surgery
I am in Billings amid a Montana heat wave.
But the day after, all the childhood drama is still there.

I am so small under a tree.
I am disappearing so fast.
Vanishing from sight.

The tree finds me.
My eyes surrender to the branches.
The branches that carry things—
leaves, birds, insects, and me.

In a sky of green I am carried.
Back to my open heart
to feast on the blessings of trees.

Author Note- Within days of writing this poem a windstorm broke several limbs from this tree. The landowner removed it from the apartment complex. I understood the rational of safety and maintenance even as my heart felt the loss. Everyday these decisions are made unknowingly of the personal connection we make with trees. In meeting the heart break, resilience and compassion are seeded. The tree lives on in my wild heart.

Inheritance

My mother died in my twenties.

To soon for me to ask her all the why's and how's-

"Why did you sacrifice a career to care for my grandmother?
Why did you marry my father? Why didn't you go to nursing
school? Why did you move the garden in 1968? Why did
you give in to the weight of doing and stop being? How did
you roll the potica dough so thin you could see right through
me?"

There was an unspoken list
of the confusing, contradictions of motherhood.

I wanted to keep her buried
but that is not the way of mothers.

It took years for me to find the gift of finding my own
answers that come from the house of vastness where she is
now.

When I feel the extinction of animals, the suffering brought on
by wars, land left barren to waste after years of abuse, the
pollution of waters, air and soil, the loss of homes human and
animal after flooding or fires.

I feel those unanswered questions
just as I remember feeling my mother.

That is how I know my mother is with me.

Helping me find the answers
in the holiness of my grief.

Seeding a New Future

Our resilience and strength as a species
is built not only on our connections
to each other but to the parts around us.

I believe the fungal network between trees
and the bond between a sapling
and a mother tree matter.

I believe that within the ecosystem
of the heart the force that keeps me alive
is in the trees too.

My blood and the sap of a tree
share a common thread that joins the sky
to a deep blue sea of joy.

I believe we were designed
to adapt and grow like a forest.
Together our connections bring harmony,
balance and growth to future generations.

My heart believes the wisdom
of a forest will uphold humans
as a new future is seeded.

Wonders

Sometimes when I fear the light is getting squeezed out
 -Drowning in a sea of unworthiness

I look to the stars and wonder
What or who is shining back?

Somewhere within the quiet of a dark night
I hear-You are alive in a world of wonder and awe.

Where else does earth, wind, water, fire and metal
create a living green planet?

It is nothing less than a miracle
that right now the mitochondria in my cells
are shining a light just like those stars

that fuels the energy
for every other process in the body.

Imagine what we could accomplish
if the world woke up to wonder.

Each moment would be witnessed as pure creativity
in a crystalline plasma of potential.
I wonder if the stars and our inner light
knew each other before birth.

I wonder if our ancestors, guardians
and guides are Stars reminding us

You are worthy of wonder.

Wild Stillness

Poems are like snow.
They blanket you in stillness.
A gentle reminder to stop
and absorb the fall.

One after another marvel of water
falls from the sky
until the whiteness reminds you
of your own brightness.

Even in the cold and dark of winter
there is a frontier to be explored.
Be still. Close your eyes—listen
to the in-between places.

Our lives are poems as are the lives
of animals, trees, mountains, flowers,
wind, and the soil beneath your feet.

In the territory of the heart
there is only one language.

Animals

An Invitation: The animals need us to wake up their beauty, to their presence, their intelligence, to their passing and to our part of the responsibility of their passing. It matters that we bring awareness and compassion to the change occurring around us. In doing so we are gifted with strength and wisdom that can only come from the heart. The animals in their passing are gifting us with an opportunity for growth that can change our future.

Facing Beauty

Three months ago white-tailed deer roamed the hills.
Going about their business of being wild
as they jumped the wire fence
before cautiously crossing the gravel road.

Long arching legs cleared the fence before landing
as precisely as any pilot coming down a runway.
The fawns came in ones and twos
hidden in grass and under trees
until their legs became strong and swift like their mothers.

I admired their presence and beauty from afar.
Taking them for granted,
as if there will always be deer.

Two months ago, we began noticing the carcasses
littered along the road and rotting in the river and fields.
The smell of death undeniable in the air as summer
heat bore down on wasting flesh.
Blue tongue and wasting disease have left a shadow
of doubt in my heart.

Will the does survive?
Will there be fawns in the spring?
Will the hills be empty of deer in the coming year?

I carry a daring kind of hope
as the face of beauty with her soft brown eyes
lands in my heart of broken things.

Bear Love

There are mothers like bears
giving generously of their ferocious love.
Nurturing growth so their young may thrive.

There are mothers confused about their power.
Slashing out in frustration and anger at their young.
They do not know that an inner tyrant is their greatest fear.

There are girls with mothers like bears
wounded by cutting words.
They lose themselves and their connection to joy.

There are women who face their mothers' fears
and claim their ferocious love before giving
that love to their mothers.

I am a woman who finds courage
in the company of bears.

Reflection

Sweet darkness in your eyes
  My eyes

Flaring breath in your nostrils
  My breath

Hooves sharp and broken by running away and running to
  My feet

Ears flat with teeth ready to tear flesh
  My words

Freedom in your tangled mane and flowing tail
  My freedom

Your dark hair and my white skin

  Reflected

Through the soft prism of our animal bodies

Full Moon in Aquarius
February 11, 2021

I open the latch to the gate
and step out into the field.
A thin blanket of fresh snow
lies underfoot.

Clouds are high and married to a cool breeze
from the north. I take the path down the hill,
passing the ponderosa pine, a monument
to a past I want to dream back into reality.
Past the hawthorn thicket and on toward the river
in hopes of a subtle change in wind chill.

A flock of thirty geese turn their eyes in my direction—
will they hear my silent request for unobtrusive passage?
One outstretched neck is followed by another
as they take a small step before gathering
their wings beneath them.
Then they ascend upward.
Another small flock on the river's edge follows.
A third flock further up the floodplain
follows the second.

Within seconds wings move in sync.
The birds come into V formation,
honking encouragement to go higher, faster.
The lead goose circles the flock back above my head
then falls back into line
as another moves forward.
The flock disappears over the valley's windblown horizon,
the sky as alive as any other wilderness.

I feel synergistic wisdom in action.
Combined efforts achieving
far more than one individual.
Here, everyone matters.
Love and beauty can fill
the emptiness of a new moon.
The planets, the geese, and I have
aligned to take flight
into the age of Love and Aquarius.

Two New Moons

I welcome the year of the water tiger.
Fluidity is meeting power.
Will the water tiger heal the earth?

I am hungry for her strength
but will she devour me
spiraling down into an unknown future?

We are at the end of a story.
Will we fight over which narrative takes its place.
Whose story is better or has more money?

Or will the tiger in me
unite with the water tiger
to ride a tidal wave of change.

Something is broken.
Can we trust the wild
tiger within to arise.

Housefly

On the pure, white innocence of this page
lands a housefly.

Black as shining coal
with wings as feathery and light as an angel.
Translucent eyes read me as I pause
my pen with curiosity.

"Oh honey," I say as jointed legs clean
the fine hairs in an up and down movement.

First one—then two—
then three legs moving
in balanced harmony.

Our eyes meet.
Not like strangers but as old friends.
I say, "Oh honey, you really need to go outside."

And then off she goes buzzing at the window.
The certainty of death outside or inside
on this late fall day.

"Oh honey," I say again, more to myself
than the fly, I love and cherish your life
as much as my own.

I pry the screen off, open the window,
and feel the cool breeze of freedom
lift us into the unknown.

Whales

Something about the comfort of entitlement
brought about a prayer to a humpback whale.
She introduced her whale self with a slap of a flipper
while whale watching in Hawaii.

The arch in the grey of her back made a subtle splash
as she surfaced with her calf. There were no words
to describe the joy felt as we breathed in unison.

The feeling ignited a memory
of the language of sonar summoned
from a deep slumber, from the bottomless blue.

My whale heard the prayer
and returned a burst of light on a wave
to my body now thousands of miles away
on the shore of the Oregon Coast.

The infant knew before any other part and opened her eyes.
The little girl laughed until she hiccupped.
The teenager let out a yell.
The young adult cried, dancing.
The mature one let go of judgment.
And everyone started to play a new tune
in sync with the whale song
sung just for me.

The Herd

On a walkabout across a parched savanna
my feet embrace this sacred earth
maybe for the first time in my adult life.

We approach herds of impala, zebra, kudzu,
and giraffe from the sunlit horizon.
We move slowly and quietly, stopping
when the herd of zebras becomes skittish

or when the impala lift their heads in unison
from their steadfast grazing. Timbu tells us
that if the giraffes find us trustworthy
the other herd animals will settle.

As my feet find a rhythm, my toes take the lead
in digging into the soft, dry ground.
This is the same earth that supported
the bushmen not that long ago.

I use my whole foot to soften the vibration of my step.
My legs follow, the hips soften. My spine stands erect.
I feed an aliveness that arouses
the soft hairs at the base of my skull.

My joy echoes across the landscape
as the impala lower their heads, the zebra settle,
the kudzu watch us from a steadfast distance,
and the giraffes stand tall, steady as any monument.

That is how my feet remember that moment—
alive but frozen, tingling with the delight of acceptance.

Suspension

Here, our group of seven, equipped with sturdy boots,
down jackets, and Sherpas to carry our packs make ready
to trek to Namche Bazaar. We begin our day respectfully,
in a line with Nepalese and foreign hikers.

Temperatures dipped below freezing overnight,
but the morning has greeted us with blue skies and a dry trail.
Prayer wheels and Mani stones anchor our journey
through Sherpa villages along the narrow valley floor.

The path—sacred, holy, historical, rugged, and beautiful.
Some parts are manicured like the Yellow Brick Road
while others are steep, rocky, and narrow. We will walk
higher and further into the thin November air.

We gaze up to soaring cliffs and snow-covered peaks.
Below us, the silt-laden waters of the Dudh Koshi River rage
on as if laughing or crying on the mountain's behalf.
The river is a constant hum as we travel upward.

A rise of 4,500 feet, seven miles, and six suspension bridges
separates us from our destination at Everest View Point.
The mountains—wild, massive, anchoring earth. Our line
stops as a pack train of yaks makes their way past us.

Behind them, two sagging, swinging parallel lines define
a suspension bridge. The last of the train of yak's sways
 in rhythm as hooves make a soft thud on steel planks.
Their backs are laden with cargo, brushing
the braided metal railing.

The yaks are orderly, well trained.
These herders speak harshly when the animals
come out of line, their words as sharp as any stick.
The bright caravan carries propane tanks,
food, and tents to the high mountain villages.

Bright, soft eyes rest between curved horns, pointing
the way to home and recovery. I watch in silence
as the strong and somber yaks disappear
down the winding trail.

The calm, sure-footed feeling of the Himalayan bovines
stays, grounding me. Dutifully, our line reassembles—
we are once again organized, autonomous, and alone
with our thoughts. The color and rhythm
of the yaks carries us upward.

Bee for Beautiful

The first time I opened the seed packet of wildflowers
tiny black seeds of Rocky Mountain Beeplant stayed
in the bag and we never met each other in the flower beds.

In the second year of wildflower planting the Beeplant hid
even deeper in the bag—I blamed the seed company.
But the third year—the tiny seeds
in the bottom of the bag came out to play.

That is how the natives are, they wait until the space
is properly prepared and the fairies can come out
to dance on long purple stalks of gratitude.

Their wings are petals of humility, the anthers long and slim
like the bodies of dancers. The seed pods wash down like
rain.
Alert and attentive I am to the flower's beauty like the bee
attracted to the inner spaces of fertility.

Oh, the action! The kind of action
only pollinators can know.
The space for X-rated stories of birds and bees.
The origin of whatever the opposite of sin is.

The fairies are electric, pulsating beings
now watching over the Beeplant.
But you must be in love with the pollinators
to hear the fairies, sing.

Dog Love Letters

Tobi wrote me a love letter
signed with a wag of his tail.
A day or two had passed before he found just the right
words to describe the heart language
carried in the curves of his long, lean, brown body.

Tobi wrote, "My heart is pumping this joyful feeling
from the tip of my nose to the end of my tail,
down to the soft pads of my paws
and into the ground beneath your feet."

The spaces between us
is elastic, allowing us to feel
each other even when we are miles apart.

Our love stretches
across continents to planets
to the solar system in our hearts.

With a lick of a tongue
the letter was sealed
and delivered in a dog beat
where it landed in my heart
to be treasured forever.

Whispers

An Invitation: Guidance comes in many forms- our dreams, a passage in a book or poem, friends, the quiet time of solitude in nature. They come as whispers-an unexpected moment of clarity or insight. Surrender to the mystery of who you are. Make these poems a soul song to deeper living to recognize your part within a bigger picture. You matter!

Beginning

When I write poetry
I see the poem as a container.
Empty space filled with ideas, memories,
and a magic that holds it all together.

When I walk in a forest
I see the trees as a container.
Bark, limbs, trunk, crown, and leaves
all shaped in emptiness.

Do trees imagine themselves as a void
for a nest, the home I live in, or the pulp for paper?
Does the unspoken, unseen essence
of a soul know its potential?

Now I see myself as a container.
The boundary of form changing
with the rhythm of days, seasons, and years.

The body is a home for a soul,
connected and separate, partial and whole.
A mystery to behold.
I imagine this is how it began.
This is the beginning.

Vespers

In your Presence
the foreground, middle ground,
and background
are one.

In your Absence
Separation, Judgment, Loss
prevail.

Failure has taught me the difference.

Surrendering to the Mystery

There is a mystery we carry within the soft folds of time.
Like a package waiting to be opened
we hold the surprise, savoring what's inside.

The suspense could topple a building.
But the mystery must be cared for with kindness.
We must show kindness to the body where awe resides.

Caring for the one who keeps looking in all
the obscured places. Until one day the looking stops
and there is no one to look to but the Self.

The Self with a capital S—residing in all things.
The shy space between the crown of trees.
The neighbor who smiles and comforts
even when he knows time is limited.
The mother pregnant with anticipation,
feeding hope to her unborn child.
The stars that roam the skies never allowing you to forget
your place on this blue planet.

We carry our caring
until wisdom tells us to open the package
to find there never was a carrier
only caring and gratitude
for the mystery we are.

Signature

The eye level of the ocean rises
and descends in waves.
What was once safe is now hidden
in a fall to swollen waters.

I am small as sand, vulnerable as an infant
in the arms of a stranger. Ground down
to the water of my existence, I face my worst fear:
I cannot swim.

The absence of gravity
forces me to anchor to something else.
I am not alone. Is the voice I hear another's?
Or is it my own?

I listen for guidance, direction,
a glimpse of a future
in a tsunami of tears.

The voice whispers, "Kick your legs. Swerve to the right."
Arms follow in rhythm. I surrender,
holding onto the edge of water's signature.

The song of the Great Ocean Mother
awakens me from a dream.
She awakens me with her vastness.

Evolution

I.
Once
a single seed
found it could break free,
and for the first time
there was a tree
that would become a forest.

High
in the mountains
a bird grabbed that seed and flew towards the sun
where the seed had to die or adapt
and become a new species of tree
that could grow in the heat.

Deep
in the intestines of a deer
that seed was infected by a virus,
and that virus changed the seed's coding
so that now the seed bore fruit
that looked like an apple.

II.
I ate that apple
and became one with it, then broke free
when the sun was so bright I had to die or adapt,
and when I caught the virus
I swam between the ripples of water

until I looked into the eyes of Christ
and saw the shadow of suffering erased,
which is how Eve rewrote history
and a new earth emerged.

Fame-Us

What do you say to the neighbor,
loved one, or friend with little time?
How do you answer the person who says,
"I don't want to go, I am not ready to die"?

What do you say to yourself when the same question
arises in yourself, in that part
that has not lived to its fullest?

What part of you is dying to be recognized—
held in life's loving arms and given a chance
to speak, to dance, to be?
To truly be here on planet earth?

Because there is no time
better than now to be
famous for being you.

I want to be famous for embodying
the fullness of flowers.
Being so desirable
no one could resist my love's nectar.

I want to be famous through my children.
For giving life and wanting nothing
in return but more life.

I want to be famous in the eyes of my dog.
For being the center of my dog's universe
And allowing him to become
just as famous in mine.

Our famous selves persist,
meeting again and again
in the deep blue shadow of cobalt stars.

The Soft Fall

Spring paints the hills green
crafting flowers with the delicate
workmanship of an artist's hand.

But autumn is wild-slinging
color across the landscape
as carelessly as any freedom fighter.

The footprint of my humanness is buried in color.
Here in the quietness of my being,
in the fall of my life, I allow myself to feel—

The sister who passed in the mid of her life.

      The unexpected death of a friend.

      The uncertainty of a future for our children.

How the recklessness of autumn
clears the cloudiness from my soul,
I do not know.

Life Is an Offering

Winter is a humble host
to invited guests
and those that wander in
with a cold gust of wind.

Winter chases summer memories
into a woolen blanket
I hold close to me as eyes drop
into an inner wellspring of stillness.

I accept winter's invitation with some reluctance
as I say farewell to the tomatoes, still green
on the vine, and the silent surrender
of petunia petals to the first frost.

Permitted use of this earth is no small thing.
So little time remains,
for life is an offering.
A debt that cannot be repaid.

I ask to be kept between this skin of earth and sky,
and in my unreadiness
I am made ready for the beauty
of true belonging.

Winter Sky

My body is a room in a house of Sky.
I was born into ancestral walls
of misunderstanding, loss, and judgment.

I built this body,
reworking Sky's gifts
to conform, survive, and "win the game."

Stories, beauty, and the raw pain
of existence fill this empty space.
Wild things come and go, offering wisdom.

Sometimes my room is bright as any shining star
and other times it collapses into darkness.
I open the door to nature during those dark times.

The Mayans and the Hopi say Sky is changing
and a new cycle is beginning.
As earth aligns with the Age of Aquarius
so a new dream state can be explored.

I wonder how my body might integrate this newness.
If humanity will be in greater harmony with Sky,
what doors might open?
What friends might be encountered?
Is equality possible with a fly on the wall
or visitors from a distant planet?

The universe is gifting Sky with greater creativity
and with it comes chaos and uncertainty.
My body senses the change and feels a readiness.

I was born to witness this new era.
For this I struggled, falling to my knees.
More than once as I looked up to Sky for help,
only to find Sky inside of me.

Crown Shyness

Shy, like the trees,
another reality
awaits at a border.

The one that we visit in our dreams.
The one aspired to when
the mind is quiet and open to receiving
bits of nothingness that spark

a sensation that dissolves into an image
with words too, and sometimes feelings.
A moment in time captured then released
so another spark has room to shine.

Like the open, shy space between the crowns
of trees, pure innocence
is grounded in the spaciousness
of all things shy and beautiful.

If I Had One More Day

If I had one more day
I would make my body a brush
and paint myself over earth's landscape
and into the hearts of all those I have loved.

All the colors and all the emotions
would be on my palette.
I would start with the earth
and paint deep, dark respectful reds
and browns for all the diversity of form.

I would paint as if my body flowed with the landscape,
matching the highs and lows,
and resting on the flat side of curves.
I would feel life flowing from the earth
with long strokes that curled and unfurled like smoke,
rising higher and higher until only open space remained.

I would feel the primal sounds of animals
bellowing forth from my mouth.
Leaping, running, crawling, slithering,
swimming, and flying onto the canvas.
Each one distinct but connected to the web of life.

For my friends, soul family and animal companions
that brought me magnitudes of growth and experiences
and brightened cloudy days, I would follow a rainbow
and then back again until double rays of color
connected us to this life and the next.

If I had one more day
I would scatter my wild beauty
into the sacredness of an eternal fire.

A Letter to the Future Guardians of This Land

I have buried rose quartz between the roots
of ancient ponderosa pines.
There are ten of them. I don't expect you to find them.
Just know they were a gift to the spirits living here.

We loved growing plants, with a special fondness
for native shrubs and trees. We grew vegetables and berries
in two gardens. One garden was near the house, the other
closer to the pond and river. Extra winter squash
was grown to feed the white-tailed deer.

In 2020, we planted the orchard of apple, pear, plum, and
cherry. All the food was grown to sustain life in the soil,
the kind of food my grandparents worked hard to grow.
Our hope was that the soil and trees would nourish you,
whoever you are.

The birds loved this property.
Several species of hawks lived in the valley, along with bald
eagles. sparrows and red-winged blackbirds were common
at the bird feeders. We grew sunflowers for the seed-eaters
and left wild thistle for the goldfinches.

There were fish in the river and a great blue heron
who lived well. Rodents were abundant
and red-tailed fox and coyotes roamed freely.
All the wildlife was welcome even as the habitat dwindled
on adjacent land as subdivisions and roads buried the hills.

We wanted the wildlife to have a home, habitat and native
food sources. Ponderosa pine, wild cherry, willow,
serviceberry, rose, even hawthorn, were planted along the
river and slopes. We watered the seedlings to give them a
good start and envisioned them mature, strong, and beautiful.

We did not give a damn about farming this land for profit.
To be in service to what is wild and untamed was the best gift
we could have given our hearts.

I have buried this note not knowing
if any of the species I write about will survive.
Not knowing if my generation will be counted
as the last to live to maturity.

Not knowing if the being who reads this is even human.

If Only Once

Plant a tree. Find a native tree
Adapted to your soil and climate.
Plant that tree where the tree guides you,
paying attention to the morning light and afternoon heat.

Choose a tree with strong and healthy roots.
Imagine those tiny roots stretching with every fiber
of their being to reach the core of the earth.
Listen to the grandmother trees
that guided you to this beginning.

Make every step a ceremony—digging the hole,
caressing the roots tenderly—and patting the soil
with reverence.

See the tree thriving—
a home for a songbird that will touch your heart
and make you look up to search for the small brown wren
singing your heart song.

Plant that tree knowing you may never
see it reach its full potential, but humans and animals
that come after you will thank the tree for being there
and in this way your soul will be graced.

Deepen the Experience

My vision for this book is that these poems will expand you, and like a wilderness take you into unknown territories. These poems are a portal in which we can see the world through the lens of the wild.

The following practices and meditations can be used by themselves or after reading the poems in this book. Allow these poems to spark a new vision that can be taken out into the world. Try them on to see how you can keep the wild alive.

How To Begin Each Day?

Do you give yourself time in the morning to wake up to this one precious day? Beginning with a ritual or a practice-like saying a word of gratitude as your feet first touch the ground-can bring awareness into the rest of the day. Make a commitment to wake up with reverence as you start your day. Being fully aware of your body, the breath, or sunlight coming through the window sets the stage for how your day unfolds. Use the poem *How to Begin Each Day* as a guide to develop your own morning practice that brings reverence to the temple of your wildness.

Have an Awe-cation

If you are reading this book, you have probably had an experience in nature or with animals that leaves you with a sense of WOW, that was amazing. Watching the sunset over the mountains after a day of walking through an old growth forest, or that perfect day on the beach with your dog. If you would like a sense of how I experience Awe read *A Forest Prayer*, *Wonders*, or *Surrendering to the Mystery*.

Take a moment to re-create one of those rich and vital memories. Re-enact the scene in your mind. What were you seeing? How did you feel? How did your body take in the beauty of the experience? Allow your mind to quiet, the body to relax and BE there. Take the scene, your feelings, the juiciness of the experience into the very depth of your cells. Stay with the felt sense for as long as you can.

Congratulations you have just performed a form of activism by generating a field of beauty and awe. The world is a better place! Your energy will now inspire others to find beauty too. In this way humanity will begin to wake up to this amazing place we call earth.

A Tree Meditation

One of the most powerful ways to connect with nature is to be in the company of trees. *A Forest Prayer, Heart Opening*, and *If Only Once* were all written from a place of love and reverence for trees.

Find a quiet place, preferably in a forest or under a tree. If the weather permits take off your shoes and plant your feet solidly on the ground. Dig your toes into the earth. You can also do this with your fingers. Imagine growing roots from your toes or hands. Sense the moisture of the earth and the texture of the soil.

Imagine the roots of your tree extending deep into the earth- so far that they reach that crystalline center. Trees send energy up the xylem and down the phloem. Step fully into your tree being and feel energy flowing up from the base of your spine and out the top of your head to the sun and then from the sun on down through the central column of the spine and back to the center of the earth.

If you feel blocks or distractions from thoughts-practice seeing them as energy and welcome them into the flow of sensations and feelings. Stay in this deeply rooted place for at least 10 minutes. When you return to your day observe how the tree energy has impacted your day.

On Warriors and Hero's

Our job as a human is to find that rare, wonderful being inside of you and share it. It takes a warrior to begin the journey. Everyone has a warrior within that can heal from trauma, resolve a difficult situation or not give into the social programming that says that is just the way it is. When that warrior comes into balance with inner peace and creativity heroes are born.

In my childhood, heroes wore capes, flew over buildings, and had Atlas like strength. My sense of heroes has changed through the years. I don't expect to find them in the limelight or up on a stage. My heroes lead with humility and kindness and care about beauty. Planting a tree, rescuing the cat in the tree, and forgiving a wrongdoing are all acts of heroism. A hero is willing to face their fears and act accordingly, in the best interest of all. *An Invitation, Lonely Warrior,* and *Facing Beauty* were written from a place of humility and courage.

What are three fears that are keeping you from claiming that wonderful heroic being inside of you? If you could find the opposite of that fear, what would it be? The opposite is often in our unconscious and when you can find and name it, there is less emotional charge and a shift in consciousness is possible. For instance, the opposite of being in control might be a facing the unknown, or the opposite of staying hidden might be being seen. Offer up the list of opposites to the universe with this simple prayer.

May the fears within me
Be transmuted into the energy of light and love
May I find courage to face the light and love
To guide me home to the peace of my inner hero.

Use this space to write, draw or make notes.

Postscript

An Invitation

The news tells us doomsday is here.
We listen to the far away tragedies as if they were our own.
The pain and wounding never cease or so it seems.

The heroes never come fast enough or strong enough to save
the day.
We numb the place that wants to care
for the high of "thank God that's not me"
and then return to the list of dos and don'ts.

Even in the dark everything is lit by a halo of light.

Every challenging situation has an element of curiosity.
When looked at from the viewpoint of a bird,
an ant, the top of a tree, or anything in nature
the perspective changes.

In the blink of an eye
tragedies become opportunities
and you become the hero you were looking for.

Our job as humans is to find that rare, wonderful
being inside of us and share it.
Waking up to that amazing you is a form of activism
and that is news worth sharing.

Acknowledgments

I wish to thank my friends and family who contributed to this collection of writing. Leaving a legacy of words that honors the wild at a time when our wilderness, our wild nature and wild animals are changing, and disappearing has inspired me to get this book completed. I am so pleased to give you the gift of these writings.

Many of these writes began as drafts in small circles in Tillamook Oregon and Pullman Washington. Thanks to all the writers who played with me in those circles and to our writing facilitators Ana Ramana and Dana Anderson. Thank you for listening to those first drafts and providing encouragement.

A deep bow to my spiritual teachers who supported me in letting go of something old so these words can shine. Special thanks to Katia Ariel and Kari Van Tine who helped with editing, graphics, and publishing. I wish to thank all things wild for their deep peace, stillness and beauty that inspired me to write this book. Special thanks to my daughter Amy and my friends and family for their encouragement. Lastly, I wish to thank my family of human and animal friends who are stars in this book. Thank you for your ongoing love and support.

www.ingramcontent.com/pod-product-compliance
Lightning Source LLC
Chambersburg PA
CBHW052025030426
42335CB00026B/3290